THiS BOOK BELONGS TO

FIND YOUR WAY THROUGH FOLSOM LET'S GO!

TO THE CiTY I CALL HOME.

A PORTiON OF THE PROCEEDS FROM THE SALE OF THiS BOOK WiLL BE DONATED TO FOLSOM-BASED NON-PROFIT ORGANiZATiONS

www.findyourwaythroughfolsom.com

Find Your Way Through Folsom
Written and Illustrated by Brian Wallace
Edited by Jessica Wallace
Published by Newport Press

NEWPORT
PRESS

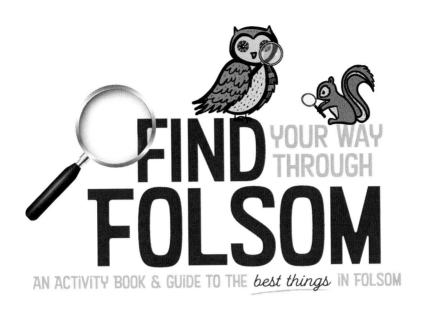

FIND YOUR WAY THROUGH FOLSOM

AN ACTIVITY BOOK & GUIDE TO THE *best things* IN FOLSOM

WRITTEN & ILLUSTRATED BY
BRIAN WALLACE

HOW TO USE THiS BOOK

Follow Folsom's most common open-space animals as they lead you to some of Folsom's best kept secrets!

EXPLORE...

Find places and things you may not know. You might need to use your smartphone to find some of the places that are highlighted in this book.

LEARN...

Learn about Folsom's history and about what makes Folsom unique.

HAVE FUN!

This book is full of activities and puzzles that will make your adventures through Folsom even more fun!

THERE ARE 6 MAGNIFYING GLASSES IN THIS BOOK!

WHEN YOU SEE THE MAGNIFYING GLASS...

There is something you should be on the lookout for!

I FOUND iT!

Draw a ☆ in the magnifying glass when you find what you are looking for!

LET'S EXPLORE!

There is a lot to see and do in Folsom.

- NATIVE AMERICANS
  Pages 3 & 4
- RANCHING & AGRICULTURE
  Pages 5 & 6
- OAK TREES
  Pages 7 & 8
- STEP BACK IN HISTORY
  Pages 9 & 10
- HISTORIC SUTTER STREET
  Pages 11 & 12

- SECRETS OF THE TRAILS
  Pages 13 & 14
- FOLSOM LAKE
  Pages 15 & 16
- ART IN FOLSOM
  Pages 17 & 18
- HAVING FUN IN FOLSOM
  Pages 19 & 20

PROTIPS!

PAGE 21 has additional info and tips to help locate the harder to find places in the book. SCAN THE QR CODE FOR AN ONLINE MAP AND CLUES.

NATiVE AMERiCANS

The southern Maidu and Nisenan people were the first to make Folsom their home.

Folsom's mild climate and location on the river provided the local residents with a variety of food, such as fruit, nuts, roots, deer, fish, and birds.

LET'S EXPLORE!

WHAT iS A GRiNDiNG ROCK?
Grinding rocks were used by the Maidu to crush acorns and prepare acorn meal.

GRiNDiNG ROCK

FiND THE MAiDU GRiNDiNG ROCK

Below the Folsom Powerhouse, at the edge of Lake Natoma, you'll see an ancient grinding rock. Look at the picture above to help you locate the grinding rock. Notice the bridge in the background.

I FOUND THE GRINDING ROCK AT LAKE NATOMA

LEARN THE MAiDU & NiSENAN WORDS FOR SUN, MOON AND WATER

ENGLiSH WORDS	MAiDU WORDS	NiSENAN WORDS
☀ Sun	Pokom	Okpajim
☾ Moon	Pōmpokom	Pombokom
◦◦◦ Water	Momim	Mom

The labyrinth is an ancient pattern found in many cultures around the world.

WOVEN BASKETS

The Maidu were excellent basket-weavers who utilized a wide variety of roots, bark, plant stems, and leaves to make baskets.

The labyrinth has only one path that leads from the outer edge to the center.

CEREMONIAL ROUNDHOUSE

BARK HOUSE

An important food source for the Maidu and Nisenan people were acorns.

RANCHING & AGRICULTURE

Folsom was once home to farmers and ranchers. Large areas of land were used to grow crops and raise livestock.

THE BRODER RANCH COMPLEX

Broder Family Homestead Park preserves the historic and cultural resources of the Broder Ranch Complex.

Here is what the home looked like

You can see where the Broder family home once stood. The footprint is outlined on the lawn with stone from the original Broder home.

LET'S EXPLORE!

FIND AN OLIVE GROVE WITH 74 HISTORIC OLIVE TREES*

In the center of Broder Family Homestead Park, you'll see olive trees that were planted by the Broder family.

THIS IS AN OLIVE PRESS!
You can see one in Broder Family Homestead Park.
FARMERS USE THIS TO PRESS OLIVES AND EXTRACT OLIVE OIL.

I FOUND THE OLIVE GROVE AT BRODER FAMILY HOMESTEAD PARK

*GREAT SPOT FOR FAMILY PORTRAITS

WORD SCRAMBLE

Unscramble the words below and discover the types of fruit commonly grown in Folsom.

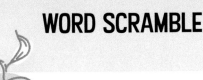

SPRGEA _ _ ⊙ _ _ _

TOPARCIS _ _ _ _ _ _ ⊙ _

PSEEHCA _ _ _ ⊙ _ _ _

SERCRHI _ ⊙ _ _ _ _ _

SELMON _ _ _ _ _ _

GIFS _ _ ⊙ _

What farm animal keeps the best time?

W ○ ○ ○ ○
    A
  D ○

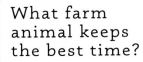

RUSSELL RANCH BARN

The Russell Ranch was a working ranch that's located in what is now Folsom's Empire Ranch neighborhood.

Materials used to build the **BARNYARD EXPERIENCE** barn at the **FOLSOM ZOO SANCTUARY** were salvaged from the Russell Ranch barn.

The Folsom Zoo Sanctuary charges a small admission fee.

OAK TREES

Many of the native oak trees in Folsom are hundreds of years old. Some of these trees, which exist in our own backyards and in parks, were the source of food, tools, heat, and shelter for the Native Americans.

Trails along **ALDER CREEK** and through the oak woodlands on the south side of Highway 50 will let you walk among native oak trees.

These oak trees are common in Folsom and they are protected.

BLUE OAKS
INTERIOR LIVE OAKS
VALLEY OAKS

LET'S EXPLORE!

FIND ONE OF THE MOST MAGNIFICENT OAK TREES IN FOLSOM*

Take Oak Avenue Parkway to North Lexington Drive. Turn right on Prewett Drive. Look for Kids Play Park.

CROSS THE STREET AND FOLLOW THE TRAIL.
LOOK FOR THE BIG OAK TREE ON YOUR RIGHT.

I FOUND THE MAGNIFICENT OAK TREE AT COHN PARK

*ALSO A GREAT SPOT FOR FAMILY PORTRAITS

WORD SEARCH

```
A R W R B A W F H E L D
S P O E H P S A C O R N
G T A O M B P E K P E K
H E L P T M A L O W K L
V P R F R S B L W E R A
M L S E U C E S Q U A C
G M C T N N A G Z A B M
O N T G K W O S D R I B
L C Z A D Q T L H D O X
B R A N C H E S T N L N
A F E W K C X F E K M W
M S E V E R G R E E N A
```

- ☐ ACORN
- ☐ LEAF
- ☐ EVERGREEN
- ☐ BARK
- ☐ BRANCHES
- ☐ TRUNK
- ☐ ROOTS
- ☐ BIRDS

Help me find the acorn!

COLOR
THE LEAF AND ACORN

Acorns and oak leaves change color. Sometimes they are green, sometimes they are brown.

What color where the oak leaves and acorns when you saw them?

HOW OLD IS THIS TREE? COUNT THE RINGS STARTING HERE AND COUNT TO THE MIDDLE.

YEARS OLD

8

STEP BACK IN HISTORY

Take a short walk through the Historic District and discover Folsom's history!

FOLLOW THE BLUE PATH AND LEARN MORE ABOUT THE RICH HISTORY OF FOLSOM!

Folsom Blvd.

Gold Lake Dr.

Reading St.

Leidesdorff Street

Sutter Street

Train Turntable

Wool Street

Scott St.

Riley Street

N NE NW W E SW SE S

START UNDER THE BRIDGE.
YOU CAN ACCESS LAKE NATOMA FROM THE END OF GOLD LAKE DRIVE.

1 GOLD RUSH

The first gold-seekers, known as 49ers, rushed to sites along the American River where the town of Folsom was founded.

African Americans were among the first to set up a mining camp. The mining camp was located across the river to the northwest.

HEAD SOUTH ON GOLD LAKE DRIVE AND CROSS THE PLAZA.

2 PONY EXPRESS

The Pony Express ran from April 1860 to October 1861 as a 10-day delivery mail service from Missouri to California.

It employed horse-mounted riders and 150 relay stations with its Western Terminus located at Folsom's Assay Office.

LOOK FOR THIS PLAQUE ON THE BUILDING. ▼

ASSAY OFFICE

3 FiRST PASSENGER RAiLROAD iN CALiFORNiA

The Sacramento Valley Railroad connected Sacramento to Folsom.

The railroad made its first official run on February 22, 1856. The 22-mile route from Sacramento to Folsom was laid out by Theodore Judah. Today, light rail runs on the same line designed by Judah.

THE TRAiN DEPOT WAS BUiLT iN 1856 AND REBUiLT iN 1906.

4 FOLSOM POWERHOUSE

In 1895, the first long-distance transmission of electricity took place at the Folsom Powerhouse. The transmission occurred over 22 miles from Folsom to Sacramento.

5 HiSTORiC TRUSS BRiDGE

$_____ FINE FOR DRIVING OVER THIS BRiDGE FASTER THAN A WALK.

Find the sign! How much is the fine?

The historic Truss Bridge opened in 1893. The bridge transported people, cattle, and vehicles across the American River. The bridge was moved to Walker, California in 1930 and moved back in Folsom in 2000.

WORD PUZZLE

Gold
Express
Powerhouse
Miners
Truss
Saddle
Missouri
Train
Dam
Folsom

10

HiSTORiC SUTTER STREET

Sutter Street has been the main street in Folsom since 1855! It has changed over the years. At one time, the road was unpaved.

Sutter Street has a long and fascinating history. It became the city's first main street when Capt. Joseph Folsom hired Theodore Judah, a surveyor and railroad engineer, to plan the town.

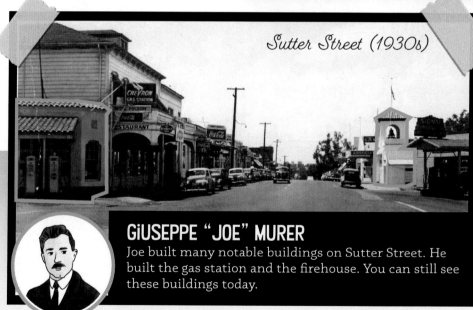

Sutter Street (1930s)

GIUSEPPE "JOE" MURER

Joe built many notable buildings on Sutter Street. He built the gas station and the firehouse. You can still see these buildings today.

SUTTER STREET UP CLOSE

Look for these things on the 700, 800, and 900 blocks of Sutter Street. Look up, down, and all around. Check the box once you find it! Do your best. If you get stuck, the online map can offer a few clues (see page 21 for more information).

SECRETS ON THE TRAILS

Take a walk or bike ride on the Folsom trails and find these unique spots! There are 50 miles of bike trails in Folsom for walking, running, hiking, and cycling.

EAST BIDWELL

BLUE RAVINE ROAD

HUMBUG CREEK

HUMBUG CREEK BIKE TRAIL

You can access the trail from the pedestrian bridge that crosses East Bidwell or from the trail entrance on Riley and Blue Ravine.

California quail are often seen on the trail.

LET'S EXPLORE!

FIND ONE OF THE MOST UNIQUE BRIDGES IN FOLSOM ON THE HUMBUG CREEK TRAIL

Between Riley Street and East Bidwell, you'll find the 300-foot Jim Konopka Volunteer Bridge – a unique wooden bridge that crosses Humbug Creek 2 times!

I FOUND THE JIM KONOPKA VOLUNTEER BRIDGE

VERNAL POOLS

Vernal pools are wetlands that fill with water in the spring and dry up in the summer. The wetlands are alive year-round and are home to wildlife and wildflowers.

YOU CAN FIND VERNAL POOLS IN FOLSOM!

If you go to the end of the street at Charlemont Place, you will see a trail that offers access to the vernal pools.

FIND THE MISSING LETTERS.

Find the missing letter in each of the trail rules to uncover the answer to the question!

Trail Rules

1. Watch your ⚪ **P E E D** when riding your bicycle

2. Keep your dog on a **L E** ⚪ **S H**

3. If you have to stop on trail: pull completely **O F** ⚪ the trail

4. Wear a **H** ⚪ **L M E T** to protect your head

6. Bike on the **R I G H** ⚪, walk on the left

6. **S T A** ⚪ on the trails to preserve the terrain and vegetation

WHY DO WE HAVE TRAIL RULES?

○ ○ ○ ○ ○ ○
1   2   3   4   5   6

OHNNY CASH TRAIL

Folsom has a trail that honors country music legend, Johnny Cash!

FOLSOM LAKE

The Folsom Lake reservoir is formed by Folsom Dam, built in 1955 to control and retain the American River.

The lake provides important flood control, hydroelectricity, drinking water, and water for irrigation.

THERE ARE SEVERAL DAY USE AREAS ON THE LAKE. CHECK OUT GRANITE BAY, BEALS POINT, FOLSOM POINT, AND BROWN'S RAVINE.

NORTH FORK - AMERICAN RIVER

SOUTH FORK - AMERICAN RIVER

FOLSOM LAKE

FOLSOM DAM

You can see the Folsom Dam by taking the **JOHNNY CASH TRAIL** over the bridge at **FOLSOM LAKE CROSSING.**

SEE THE WiLDFLOWERS!

Taking a short hike at Folsom Lake in the spring is a great time to see wildflowers.

LET'S EXPLORE!

FiND WiLDFLOWERS ON THE SHORES OF FOLSOM LAKE

The wildflowers are in bloom in April and May. The wildflower bloom depends on the weather.

I FOUND THE WILDFLOWERS AT FOLSOM LAKE

LET'S GO ON A NATURE HiKE

See how many things you can find. If you don't find everything this time, bring your checklist next time!

- ☐ Feather
- ☐ Acorn
- ☐ Footprint
- ☐ Heart-shaped rock
- ☐ Spider web
- ☐ Squirrel
- ☐ Tree stump
- ☐ Plant with flowers or berries
- ☐ Flying insect
- ☐ Boat
- ☐ Animal tracks
- ☐ Bird flying overhead

Let's find the **POPPiES!**

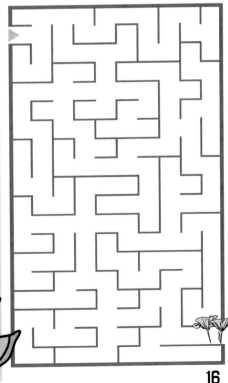

ART iN FOLSOM

On this short **1-MiLE WALK**, you'll see several pieces of public art.

Folsom has a diverse and growing collection of public art! Public art can be found throughout the city and enhances public spaces.

LET'S EXPLORE!

FiND THE PUBLiC ART iN THE NATOMA STATiON NEiGHBORHOOD

Start at Bigfoot Mini Park.
Follow Turnpike Drive to Boxcar Way.
Deer/Rabbit Mini Park will be on your left.

I FOUND THE ARTWORK iN THE NATOMA STATiON NEiGHBORHOOD

FOLLOW THE CLUES TO FiND THE PiECES OF PUBLiC ART.

Look around and use the clues below to find the public art.

ART AT BiGFOOT MiNi PARK

Find the sculpture with two big feet.

☐ **FOUND IT!**

Stephen Kaltenbach
Brazen
(1990)

Find the mural with a snake on it.

☐ **FOUND IT!**

James Melchert
Flows
(1990)

Find the sculpture with insects.

☐ **FOUND IT!**

Robert Brady
Brood
(1990)

NOW, LET'S HEAD TO DEER/RABBIT MiNi PARK

Find the sculpture
with two big ears.

☐ **FOUND IT!**

Donna Billick
Jack and Jillian Rabbit
(1990)

There are 2 of us.
Find us both.

☐ **FOUND THEM!**

Roger Berry
Gaze
(1990)

WHERE'S THE REST?

Imagine what the sculpture
"Brazen" might look like if
it had arms, a head and a
body. Be creative!

CREATE A MURAL

Create a mural that highlights
something special about Folsom.

HAVING FUN IN FOLSOM!

There is a lot to do in Folsom! Here are a few things you might want to try.

SPLASH AROUND!

Beat the heat and head over to one of Folsom's 3 spray parks. There is a flume and creek water feature at Livermore Community Park, and splash pads at Kemp Park and Nisenan Park. Spray parks are typically open from late May through late September.

THE WATER FEATURE AT LIVERMORE COMMUNITY PARK

Give it a try! It's free!

LET'S PLAY DISC GOLF

Disc golf is a game the whole family can enjoy. It's a lot like regular golf, but instead of a ball, you throw a disc. Instead of a hole, your target is a basket.

B.T. Collins Park in Folsom has a 18-basket course and a practice area for new disc golfers!

CHECK OUT THE BiKE PARK AND SKATE PARK

The bike park features include jumps, banks, rollers, and a tabletop!

The skate park is great for street-style boarding and scooters. The park features grinding rails, boxes, and bowls.

EXPLORE HiNKLE CREEK NATURE AREA

Take an easy 1-mile hike along Hinkle Creek. You will find bridges, climbing rocks, and native plants!

KAYAK OR CATCH A FISH AT WiLLOW HiLL RESERVOiR

Willow Hill Reservoir is a fun spot to hike, kayak, or go fishing. Not many people know about this hidden gem.

PROTiPS!

Here are a few tips if you are heading out to explore Folsom!

NEED A LiTTLE HELP? CHECK OUT THE MAP!

www.findyourwaythroughfolsom.com/map

NOT SURE HOW TO FiND SOME OF THE PLACES iN THE BOOK? Most places can be found on a map.

NATiVE AMERiCANS
Pages 3 & 4

The grinding rock is on the banks of Lake Natoma. You have to enter the Folsom Powerhouse State Park and follow the trail to the water. There are also grinding rocks at Hinkle Creek.

RANCHiNG & AGRiCULTURE
Pages 5 & 6

Broder Family Homestead Park is a great place to reconnect with Folsom's past. Interpretive signs help in imagining what life was like on the farm. There is also evidence of Folsom's ranching heritage near the White Rock Springs neighborhood.

GOiNG FOR A HiKE?

Wear comfortable shoes, bring water and a small snack, wear a hat and sunscreen. And bring bug spray.

OAK TREES
Pages 7 & 8

There are several places in Folsom where you can walk among the oak trees. Some of the best oaks are at B.T. Collins Park, Cohn Park, Hinkle Creek, and on the south side of Highway 50.

STEP BACK IN HISTORY
Pages 9 & 10

A short walk around the Historic District will expose you to the rich history of Folsom. Check out Pioneer Village or Folsom History Museum for a deeper dive into Folsom's past.

HISTORIC SUTTER STREET
Pages 11 & 12

Small town charm and history around every corner. The activity on page 12 will take you on a fun tour of Sutter Street. Have a look down Sutter Street crossing Riley and compare your view to the old photos on page 11.

SECRETS OF THE TRAILS
Pages 13 & 14

There are 50 miles of trails in Folsom and many of the trails are Class 1 bike paths. To access the bridge referenced on page 13, you can access the trail from Riley or East Bidwell Street.

FOLSOM LAKE
Pages 15 & 16

Folsom Lake is a great place for recreation and exploring. There is a day-use fee at all Folsom Recreation Area day-use areas.

ART IN FOLSOM
Pages 17 & 18

Folsom has a large public art collection. The largest concentration of public art is in the Natoma Station neighborhood. See the full collection at folsompresents.com.

HAVING FUN IN FOLSOM
Pages 19 & 20

Folsom city parks offer endless options for fun. Folsom also has a great public library, an art gallery, and a zoo sanctuary.

MORE ACTIVITIES AND PUZZLES

LET'S DRAW!

Draw what you see in the boxes. The easiest way to draw something is to work in smaller sections.

FIND THE DIFFERENCES

There are 8 differences in picture Ⓐ and picture Ⓑ.

Can you find the differences?

LET'S WRITE A
SiLLY STORY

Fill in the blanks with a friend. Don't read the silly story until your friend has given you words for all the blanks.

The Pony Express was a _____ way of
Adjective

delivering mail across the _____ American
Adjective

frontier in the 1800s. Riders would _____ on
Verb

their _____ horses from station to station,
Adjective

braving _____ weather and _____
Adjective Adjective

terrain to make sure that letters and packages

reached their destination on time. One famous

rider, named _____, was known for his
Proper Noun

_____ speed and _____ bravery.
Adjective Adjective

Despite the dangers of the job, the Pony Express was

a _____ success, delivering mail from
Adjective

_____ to _____ in just
Proper Noun Proper Noun

_____ days!
Number

23

HiDDEN PiCTURES

Find these hidden items in the picture below.
You can color this page too.

FIND THE MATCH!

Draw a line to connect the matching trees and leaves.

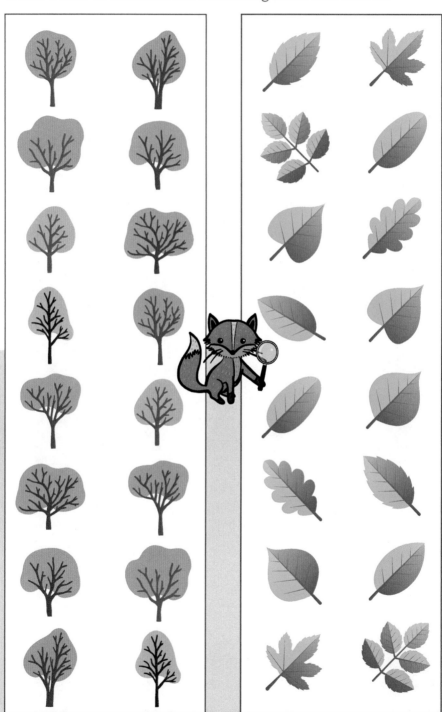

MY FOLSOM FAVORITES!

♥ 95630

DATE :

MY FAVORITE THING TO DO IN FOLSOM IS

MY FAVORITE PLACE TO GO IN FOLSOM IS

MY FAVORITE PLACE TO EAT IN FOLSOM IS

MY FAVORITE PLACE FOR DESSERT IN FOLSOM IS

MY FAVORITE PARK IN FOLSOM IS

MY FAVORITE PLACE TO GO FOR A WALK IN FOLSOM IS

FIND YOUR WAY THROUGH FOLSOM

NOTES

DATE :

ABOUT THiS BOOK

This book is a celebration of the city I've called home for the last 20 years!

Hopefully, you'll find some things in this book that you didn't know about!

Folsom has a rich history and unique opportunities to connect with nature.

The animals in this book are our neighbors and live in the open spaces that back up to our neighborhoods.

I hope you enjoy this book and discover new things on your adventures.

Author/Illustrator of
FiND YOUR WAY THROUGH FOLSOM,
Brian Wallace

As a long-time Folsom resident, I appreciate the work that our local non-profit organizations are doing within our community. I will be donating a portion of the proceeds from the sale of this book to a different non-profit on a quarterly basis.

A special
THANK YOU!

I want to express my appreciation for my family – Jess, Cole, and Claire. Thank you for your encouragement and support.

I'd also like to thank Erik Schmid (Red Bus Brewing Company) and Stacy Gould (Ruby's Books) for supporting me and my creative endeavors.

Published by NEWPORT PRESS

OTHER BOOKS WRITTEN AND iLLUSTRATED BY BRiAN WALLACE

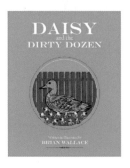

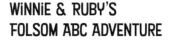

DAiSY AND THE DiRTY DOZEN

Daisy and the Dirty Dozen is the true and heartwarming story of a mallard duck and her 12 ducklings that make their home in a suburban family's swimming pool.

You can see the real-life Daisy and the Dirty Dozen at www.daisyandthedirtydozen.com

WiNNiE & RUBY'S FOLSOM ABC ADVENTURE

Winnie and Ruby's Folsom ABC Adventure is an alphabetical adventure through the city of Folsom. Each page of the book highlights the best things about Folsom, from A to Z!

This book features two of Folsom's most famous animal friends, Winnie (the Sutter Street pig) and Ruby (Ruby's Books).

Learn more about the author & illustrator of
FiND YOUR WAY THROUGH FOLSOM at www.brianwallaceart.com

BRIAN WALLACE ART

THE ART OF BRIAN WALLACE

Made in the USA
Columbia, SC
05 March 2023

13080621R00020